COPYRIGHT BASICS

Produced by George Davis.

Copyright Basics (Circular 1)

U.S. Copyright Office - Library of Congress

Copyright Basics
September 2000
——————————————————————— Copyright Basics ———————————————————————

(See Format Note at end of document.)

Table of Contents

+ Application Forms
+ Fill-in Forms
+ Fees
+ Search of Copyright Office Records
+ For Further Information

WHAT IS COPYRIGHT?

Copyright is a form of protection provided by the laws of the United States (title 17, U.S. Code) to the authors of "original works of authorship", including literary, dramatic, musical, artistic, and certain other intellectual works. This protection is available to both published and unpublished works. Section 106 of the 1976 Copyright Act generally gives the owner of copyright the exclusive right to do and to authorize others to do the following:

+ *To reproduce* the work in copies or phonorecords;

+ To prepare *derivative works* based upon the work;

  + *To distribute copies or phonorecords* of the work to the public by
    sale or other transfer of ownership, or by rental, lease, or
    lending;
  + To perform the work publicly, in the case of literary, musical,
    dramatic, and choreographic works, pantomimes, and motion pictures
    and other audiovisual works;
+ *To display the copyrighted work publicly*, in the case of literary, musical, dramatic, and choreographic works, pantomimes, and pictorial, graphic, or sculptural works, including the individual images of a motion picture or other audiovisual work; and

+ In the case of *sound recordings, to perform the work publicly* by means of a *digital audio transmission*.

In addition, certain authors of works of visual art have the rights of attribution and integrity as described in Title 17, Chap 1, Section 106a (Circular 92) of the 1976 Copyright Act. For further information, request "Copyright Registration for Works of the Visual Arts" [http://www.loc.gov/copyright/circs/circ40.pdf].

It is illegal for anyone to violate any of the rights provided by the copyright law to the owner of copyright. These rights, however, are not unlimited in scope.

Title 17, Chap 1 of the 1976 Copyright Act establish limitations on these rights. In some cases, these limitations are specified exemptions from copyright liability. One major limitation is the doctrine of "fair use", which is given a statutory basis in Title 17, Chap1, Section 107 of the 1976 Copyright Act. In other instances, the limitation takes the form of a "compulsory license" under which certain limited uses of copyrighted works are permitted upon payment of specified royalties and compliance with statutory conditions. For further information about the limitations of any of these rights, consult the copyright law or write to the Copyright Office.

———————————————————————————— WHO CAN CLAIM COPYRIGHT

Copyright protection subsists from the time the work is created in fixed form. The copyright in the work of authorship *immediately* becomes the property of the author who created the work. Only the author or those deriving their rights through the author can rightfully claim copyright.

In the case of works made for hire, the employer and not the employee is considered to be the author. Title 17, Chap 1, Sec. 101 of the copyright law defines a "work made for hire" as:

+ (1) a work prepared by an employee within the scope of his or her employment; or

  + (2) a work specially ordered or commissioned for use as:
   + a contribution to a collective work
   + a part of a motion picture or other audiovisual work
   + a translation
   + a supplementary work
   + a compilation
   + an instructional text
   + a test
   + answer material for a test
   + a sound recording
   + an atlas
if the parties expressly agree in a written instrument signed by them that the work shall be considered a work made for hire….

The authors of a joint work are co-owners of the copyright in the work, unless there is an agreement to the contrary.

Copyright in each separate contribution to a periodical or other collective work is distinct from copyright in the collective work as a whole and vests initially with the author of the contribution.

Two General Principles

+ Mere ownership of a book, manuscript, painting, or any other copy or phonorecord does not give the possessor the copyright. The law provides that transfer of ownership of any material object that embodies a protected work does not of itself convey any rights in the copyright.

+ Minors may claim copyright, but state laws may regulate the business dealings involving copyrights owned by minors. For information on relevant state laws, consult an attorney.

——————— COPYRIGHT AND NATIONAL ORIGIN OF THE WORK

Copyright protection is available for all unpublished works, regardless of the nationality or domicile of the author. Published works are eligible for copyright protection in the United States if *any* one of the following conditions is met:

+ On the date of first publication, one or more of the authors is a national or domiciliary of the United States, or is a national, domiciliary, or sovereign authority of a treaty party,* or is a stateless person wherever that person may be domiciled; or *A treaty party is a country or intergovernmental organization other than the United States that is a party to an international agreement.

+ The work is first published in the United States or in a foreign nation that, on the date of first publication, is a treaty party. For purposes of this condition, a work that is published in the United States or a treaty party within 30 days after publication in a foreign nation that is not a treaty party shall be considered to be first published in the United States or such treaty party, as the case may be; or

+ The work is a sound recording that was first fixed in a treaty party; or

+ The work is a pictorial, graphic, or sculptural work that is incorporated in a building or other structure, or an architectural work that is embodied in a building and the building or structure is located in the United States or a treaty party; or

  + The work is first published by the United Nations or any of its

specialized agencies, or by the Organization of American States; or
+ The work is a foreign work that was in the public domain in the
  United States prior to 1996 and its copyright was restored under the
  Uruguay Round Agreements Act (URAA). Request "Highlights of
  Copyright Amendments Contained in the Uruguay Round Agreements Act
  (URAA-GATT), [http://www.loc.gov/copyright/circs/circ38b.pdf], for
  further information.
+ The work comes within the scope of a Presidential proclamation.

WHAT WORKS ARE PROTECTED?

Copyright protects "original works of authorship" that are fixed in a tangible
form of expression. The fixation need not be directly perceptible so long as it
may be communicated with the aid of a machine or device. Copyrightable
works include the following categories:

+ (1) literary works; + (2) musical works, including any accompanying words
+ (3) dramatic works, including any accompanying music + (4) pantomimes
and choreographic works + (5) pictorial, graphic, and sculptural works + (6)
motion pictures and other audiovisual works + (7) sound recordings + (8)
architectural works

These categories should be viewed broadly. For example, computer programs
and most "compilations" may be registered as "literary works"; maps and
architectural plans may be registered as "pictorial, graphic, and sculptural
works."

WHAT IS NOT PROTECTED BY COPYRIGHT?

Several categories of material are generally not eligible for federal copyright
protection. These include among others:

+ Works that have *not* been fixed in a tangible form of expression (for
example, choreographic works that have not been notated or recorded, or
improvisational speeches or performances that have not been written or
recorded)

  + Titles, names, short phrases, and slogans; familiar symbols or

designs; mere variations of typographic ornamentation, lettering, or
coloring; mere listings of ingredients or contents
+ Ideas, procedures, methods, systems, processes, concepts,
principles, discoveries, or devices, as distinguished from a
description, explanation, or illustration
+ Works consisting *entirely* of information that is common property and
containing no original authorship (for example: standard calendars, height and
weight charts, tape measures and rulers, and lists or tables taken from public
documents or other common sources)

HOW TO SECURE A COPYRIGHT

Copyright Secured Automatically upon Creation

The way in which copyright protection is secured is frequently misunderstood.
No publication or registration or other action in the Copyright Office is
required to secure copyright. (See following Note.) There are, however, certain
definite advantages to registration. See "Copyright Registration." Copyright is
secured *automatically* when the work is created, and a work is "created"
when it is fixed in a copy or phonorecord for the first time. "Copies" are
material objects from which a work can be read or visually perceived either
directly or with the aid of a machine or device, such as books, manuscripts,
sheet music, film, videotape, or microfilm. "Phonorecords" are material objects
embodying fixations of sounds (excluding, by statutory definition, motion
picture soundtracks), such as cassette tapes, CDs, or LPs. Thus, for example, a
song (the "work") can be fixed in sheet music (" copies") or in phonograph
disks (" phonorecords"), or both.

If a work is prepared over a period of time, the part of the work that is fixed
on a particular date constitutes the created work as of that date.

PUBLICATION

Publication is no longer the key to obtaining federal copyright as it was under
the Copyright Act of 1909. However, publication remains important to
copyright owners.

The 1976 Copyright Act defines publication as follows:

"Publication" is the distribution of copies or phonorecords of a work to the public by sale or other transfer of ownership, or by rental, lease, or lending. The offering to distribute copies or phonorecords to a group of persons for purposes of further distribution, public performance, or public display constitutes publication. A public performance or display of a work does not of itself constitute publication.

***

NOTE: Before 1978, federal copyright was generally secured by the act of publication with notice of copyright, assuming compliance with all other relevant statutory conditions. U. S. works in the public domain on January 1, 1978, (for example, works published without satisfying all conditions for securing federal copyright under the Copyright Act of 1909) remain in the public domain under the 1976 Copyright Act.

Certain foreign works originally published without notice had their copyrights restored under the Uruguay Round Agreements Act (URAA). Request Circular 38B [http://www.loc.gov/copyright/circs/circ38b.pdf] and see the "Notice of Copyright" section of this publication for further information.

Federal copyright could also be secured before 1978 by the act of registration in the case of certain unpublished works and works eligible for ad interim copyright. The 1976 Copyright Act automatically extends to full term (Title 17, Chap. 3, Sec. 304 sets the term) copyright for all works, including those subject to ad interim copyright if ad interim registration has been made on or before June 30, 1978.

***

A further discussion of the definition of "publication" can be found in the legislative history of the 1976 Copyright Act. The legislative reports define "to the public" as distribution to persons under no explicit or implicit restrictions with respect to disclosure of the contents. The reports state that the definition makes it clear that the sale of phonorecords constitutes publication of the underlying work, for example, the musical, dramatic, or literary work embodied in a phonorecord. The reports also state that it is clear that any form of dissemination in which the material object does not change hands, for example, performances or displays on television, is *not* a publication no matter how many people are exposed to the work. However, when copies or phonorecords are offered for sale or lease to a group of wholesalers, broadcasters, or motion picture theaters, publication does take place if the purpose is further distribution, public performance, or public display.

Publication is an important concept in the copyright law for several reasons:

  + Works that are published in the United States are subject to
    mandatory deposit with the Library of Congress. See discussion on
    "Mandatory Deposit for Works Published in the United States."
  + Publication of a work can affect the limitations on the exclusive
    rights of the copyright owner that are set forth in Title 17, Chap 1
    of the law.
+ The year of publication may determine the duration of copyright protection for anonymous and pseudonymous works (when the author's identity is not revealed in the records of the Copyright Office) and for works made for hire.

+ Deposit requirements for registration of published works differ from those for registration of unpublished works. See discussion on "Registration Procedures."

+ When a work is published, it may bear a notice of copyright to identify the year of publication and the name of the copyright owner and to inform the public that the work is protected by copyright. Copies of works published before March 1, 1989, must bear the notice or risk loss of copyright protection. See discussion on "Notice of Copyright" below.

NOTICE OF COPYRIGHT

The use of a copyright notice is no longer required under U. S. law, although it is often beneficial. Because prior law did contain such a requirement, however, the use of notice is still relevant to the copyright status of older works.

Notice was required under the 1976 Copyright Act. This requirement was eliminated when the United States adhered to the Berne Convention, effective March 1, 1989. Although works published without notice before that date could have entered the public domain in the United States, the Uruguay Round Agreements Act (URAA) restores copyright in certain foreign works originally published without notice. For further information about copyright amendments in the URAA, request Circular 38 [http://www.loc.gov/copyright/circs/circ38b.pdf] .

The Copyright Office does not take a position on whether copies of works first published with notice before March 1, 1989, which are distributed on or after March 1, 1989, must bear the copyright notice.

Use of the notice may be important because it informs the public that the work is protected by copyright, identifies the copyright owner, and shows the year of first publication. Furthermore, in the event that a work is infringed, if a proper notice of copyright appears on the published copy or copies to which a defendant in a copyright infringement suit had access, then no weight shall be given to such a defendant's interposition of a defense based on innocent infringement in mitigation of actual or statutory damages, except as provided in Title 17, Chap. 5, Sec. 504 of the copyright law. Innocent infringement occurs when the infringer did not realize that the work was protected.

The use of the copyright notice is the responsibility of the copyright owner and does not require advance permission from, or registration with, the Copyright Office.

Form of Notice for Visually Perceptible Copies

The notice for visually perceptible copies should contain all the following three elements:

1. The symbol (the letter C in a circle), or the word "Copyright," or the abbreviation "Copr."; and

2. The year of first publication of the work. In the case of compilations or derivative works incorporating previously published material, the year date of first publication of the compilation or derivative work is sufficient. The year date may be omitted where a pictorial, graphic, or sculptural work, with accompanying textual matter, if any, is reproduced in or on greeting cards, postcards, stationery, jewelry, dolls, toys, or any useful article; and

3. The name of the owner of copyright in the work, or an abbreviation by which the name can be recognized, or a generally known alternative designation of the owner.

Example: (the letter C in a circle symbol) 2000 John Doe

The "C in a circle" notice is used only on "visually perceptible copies." Certain kinds of works—for example, musical, dramatic, and literary works—may be fixed not in "copies" but by means of sound in an audio recording. Since audio recordings such as audio tapes and phonograph disks are "phonorecords" and not "copies," the "C in a circle" notice is not used to indicate protection of the underlying musical, dramatic, or literary work that is recorded.

Form of Notice for Phonorecords of Sound Recordings*

* Sound recordings are defined in the law as "works that result from the fixation of a series of musical, spoken, or other sounds, but not including the sounds accompanying a motion picture or other audiovisual work." Common examples include recordings of music, drama, or lectures. A sound recording is not the same as a phonorecord. A phonorecord is the physical object in which works of authorship are embodied. The word "phonorecord" includes cassette tapes, CDs, LPs, 45 r. p. m. disks, as well as other formats.

The notice for phonorecords embodying a sound recording should contain all the following three elements:

1. *The symbol* (the letter P in a circle); and

2. *The year of first publication* of the sound recording; and

3. *The name of the owner of copyright* in the sound recording, or an abbreviation by which the name can be recognized, or a generally known alternative designation of the owner. If the producer of the sound recording is named on the phonorecord label or container and if no other name appears in conjunction with the notice, the producer's name shall be considered a part of the notice.

Example: (the letter P in a circle symbol) 2000 A. B. C. Records Inc.

NOTE: Since questions may arise from the use of variant forms of the notice, you may wish to seek legal advice before using any form of the notice other than those given here.

Position of Notice

The copyright notice should be affixed to copies or phonorecords in such a way as to "give reasonable notice of the claim of copyright." The three elements of the notice should ordinarily appear together on the copies or phonorecords or on the phonorecord label or container. The Copyright Office has issued regulations concerning the form and position of the copyright notice in the

Code   of   Federal   Regulations   (
[http://www.loc.gov/copyright/title37/201/37cfr201.20.html]). For more
information, request [http://www.loc.gov/copyright/circs/circ03.pdf] ,
"Copyright Notice."

-=Publications Incorporating U. S. Government Works=-

Works by the U. S. Government are not eligible for U. S. copyright protection.
For works published on and after March 1, 1989, the previous notice
requirement for works consisting primarily of one or more U. S. Government
works has been eliminated. However, use of a notice on such a work will defeat
a claim of innocent infringement as previously described provided the notice
also includes a statement that identifies either those portions of the work in
which copyright is claimed or those portions that constitute U. S. Government
material.

Example: (the letter C in a circle symbol) 2000 Jane Brown. Copyright claimed
in Chapters 7-10, exclusive of U. S. Government maps

Copies of works published before March 1, 1989, that consist primarily of one
or more works of the U. S. Government *should* have a notice and the
identifying statement.

-=Unpublished Works=-

The author or copyright owner may wish to place a copyright notice on any
unpublished copies or phonorecords that leave his or her control. _ Example:
Unpublished work (letter C in a circle symbol) 1999 Jane Doe

-=Omission of the Notice and Errors in Notice=-

The 1976 Copyright Act attempted to ameliorate the strict consequences of
failure to include notice under prior law. It contained provisions that set out
specific corrective steps to cure omissions or certain errors in notice. Under
these provisions, an applicant had 5 years after publication to cure omission of
notice or certain errors. Although these provisions are technically still in the
law, their impact has been limited by the amendment making notice optional
for all works published on and after March 1, 1989. For further information,
request Circular 3 [http://www.loc.gov/copyright/circs/circ03.pdf].

HOW LONG COPYRIGHT PROTECTION ENDURES

Works Originally Created on or after January 1, 1978

A work that is created (fixed in tangible form for the first time) on or after January 1, 1978, is automatically protected from the moment of its creation and is ordinarily given a term enduring for the author's life plus an additional 70 years after the author's death. In the case of "a joint work prepared by two or more authors who did not work for hire," the term lasts for 70 years after the last surviving author's death. For works made for hire, and for anonymous and pseudonymous works (unless the author's identity is revealed in Copyright Office records), the duration of copyright will be 95 years from publication or 120 years from creation, whichever is shorter.

Works Originally Created before January 1, 1978, But Not Published or Registered by That Date
These works have been automatically brought under the statute and are now given federal copyright protection. The duration of copyright in these works will generally be computed in the same way as for works created on or after January 1, 1978: the life-plus-70 or 95/120-year terms will apply to them as well. The law provides that in no case will the term of copyright for works in this category expire before December 31, 2002, and for works published on or before December 31, 2002, the term of copyright will not expire before December 31, 2047.

Works Originally Created and Published or Registered before January 1, 1978

Under the law in effect before 1978, copyright was secured either on the date a work was published with a copyright notice or on the date of registration if the work was registered in unpublished form. In either case, the copyright endured for a first term of 28 years from the date it was secured. During the last (28th) year of the first term, the copyright was eligible for renewal. The Copyright Act of 1976 extended the renewal term from 28 to 47 years for copyrights that were subsisting on January 1, 1978, or for pre-1978 copyrights restored under the Uruguay Round Agreements Act (URAA), making these works eligible for a total term of protection of 75 years. Public Law 105-298 [http://thomas.loc.gov/cgi-bin/bdquery/z?d105:SN00505:
|TOM:/bss/d105query.html|], enacted on October 27, 1998, further extended the renewal term of copyrights still subsisting on that date by an additional 20 years, providing for a renewal term of 67 years and a total term of protection of 95 years.

Public Law 102-307 [http://thomas.loc.gov/cgi-bin/bdquery/z?d102:SN00756:|TOM:/bss/d102query.html||] enacted on June 26, 1992, amended the 1976 Copyright Act to provide for automatic renewal of the term of copyrights secured between January 1, 1964, and December 31, 1977. Although the renewal term is automatically provided, the Copyright Office does not issue a renewal certificate for these works unless a renewal application and fee are received and registered in the Copyright Office.

Public Law 102-307 [http://thomas.loc.gov/cgi-bin/bdquery/z?d102:SN00756:|TOM:/bss/d102query.html||] makes renewal registration optional. Thus, filing for renewal registration is no longer required in order to extend the original 28- year copyright term to the full 95 years. However, some benefits accrue from making a renewal registration during the 28th year of the original term.

For more detailed information on renewal of copyright and the copyright term, request "Renewal of Copyright" [http://www.loc.gov/copyright/circs/circ15.pdf] ; "Duration of Copyright" [http://www.loc.gov/copyright/circs/circ15a.pdf]; and "Extension of Copyright Terms" [http://www.loc.gov/copyright/circs/circ15t.pdf].

TRANSFER OF COPYRIGHT

Any or all of the copyright owner's *exclusive* rights or any subdivision of those rights may be transferred, but the transfer of exclusive rights is not valid unless that transfer is in writing and signed by the owner of the rights conveyed or such owner's duly authorized agent. Transfer of a right on a nonexclusive basis does not require a written agreement.

A copyright may also be conveyed by operation of law and may be bequeathed by will or pass as personal property by the applicable laws of intestate succession.

Copyright is a personal property right, and it is subject to the various state laws and regulations that govern the ownership, inheritance, or transfer of personal property as well as terms of contracts or conduct of business. For information about relevant state laws, consult an attorney.

Transfers of copyright are normally made by contract. The Copyright Office does not have any forms for such transfers. The law does provide for the recordation in the Copyright Office of transfers of copyright ownership. Although recordation is not required to make a valid transfer between the parties, it does provide certain legal advantages and may be required to validate the transfer as against third parties. For information on recordation of transfers and other documents related to copyright, request "Recordation of Transfers and Other Documents" [http://www.loc.gov/copyright/circs/circ12.pdf].

Termination of Transfers

Under the previous law, the copyright in a work reverted to the author, if living, or if the author was not living, to other specified beneficiaries, provided a renewal claim was registered in the 28th year of the original term.* The present law drops the renewal feature except for works already in the first term of statutory protection when the present law took effect. Instead, the present law permits termination of a grant of rights after 35 years under certain conditions by serving written notice on the transferee within specified time limits.

*The copyright in works eligible for renewal on or after June 26, 1992, will vest in the name of the renewal claimant on the effective date of any renewal registration made during the 28th year of the original term. Otherwise, the renewal copyright will vest in the party entitled to claim renewal as of December 31st of the 28th year.

For works already under statutory copyright protection before 1978, the present law provides a similar right of termination covering the newly added years that extended the former maximum term of the copyright from 56 to 95 years. For further information, request Circular 15a [http://www.loc.gov/copyright/circs/circ15a.pdf] and Circular 15t [http://www.loc.gov/copyright/circs/circ15t.pdf] .

INTERNATIONAL COPYRIGHT PROTECTION

There is no such thing as an "international copyright" that will automatically protect an author's writings throughout the entire world. Protection against unauthorized use in a particular country depends, basically, on the national laws of that country. However, most countries do offer protection to foreign works under certain conditions, and these conditions have been greatly simplified by international copyright treaties and conventions. For further information and a list of countries that maintain copyright relations with the United States, request "International Copyright Relations of the United States." [http://www.loc.gov/copyright/circs/circ38a.pdf].

COPYRIGHT REGISTRATION

In general, copyright registration is a legal formality intended to make a public record of the basic facts of a particular copyright. However, registration is not a condition of copyright protection. Even though registration is not a requirement for protection, the copyright law provides several inducements or advantages to encourage copyright owners to make registration. Among these advantages are the following:

+ Registration establishes a public record of the copyright claim.

+ Before an infringement suit may be filed in court, registration is necessary for works of U. S. origin.

+ If made before or within 5 years of publication, registration will establish prima facie evidence in court of the validity of the copyright and of the facts stated in the certificate.

+ If registration is made within 3 months after publication of the work or prior to an infringement of the work, statutory damages and attorney's fees will be available to the copyright owner in court actions. Otherwise, only an award of actual damages and profits is available to the copyright owner.

+ Registration allows the owner of the copyright to record the registration with the U. S. Customs Service for protection against the importation of infringing copies. For additional information, request Publication No. 563 "How to Protect Your Intellectual Property Right," from: U.S. Customs Service, P.O. Box 7404, Washington, D.C. 20044. See the U.S. Customs Service Website at [http://www.customs.gov] for online publications.

Registration may be made at any time within the life of the copyright. Unlike the law before 1978, when a work has been registered in unpublished form, it is not necessary to make another registration when the work becomes published, although the copyright owner may register the published edition, if desired.

REGISTRATION PROCEDURES

Original Registration

To register a work, send the following three elements *in the same envelope or package* to:

Library of Congress
Copyright Office
101 Independence Avenue, S.E.
Washington, D.C. 20559-6000
1. A properly completed application form. 2. A nonrefundable filing fee of $30 (effective through June 30, 2002) for each application.

NOTE: Copyright Office fees are subject to change. For current fees, please check the Copyright Office Website at [http://www.loc.gov/copyright/] write the Copyright Office, or call (202) 707-3000.

3. A nonreturnable deposit of the work being registered. The deposit requirements vary in particular situations. The general requirements follow.

Also note the information under "Special Deposit Requirements."

 + If the work was first published in the United States on or after
   January 1, 1978, two complete copies or phonorecords of the best
   edition.
 + If the work was first published in the United States before January
   1, 1978, two complete copies or phonorecords of the work as first
   published.
 + If the work was first published outside the United States, one
   complete copy or phonorecord of the work as first published.
+ If sending multiple works, all applications, deposits, and fees should be sent in the same package. If possible, applications should be attached to the appropriate deposit. Whenever possible, number each package (e. g., 1 of 3, 2 of 4) to facilitate processing.

What Happens if the Three Elements Are Not Received Together

Applications and fees received without appropriate copies, phonorecords, or identifying material will not be processed and ordinarily will be returned. Unpublished deposits without applications or fees ordinarily will be returned, also. In most cases, published deposits received without applications and fees can be immediately transferred to the collections of the Library of Congress. This practice is in accordance with Title 17, Chap. 4, Sec. 408 of the law, which provides that the published deposit required for the collections of the Library of Congress may be used for registration only if the deposit is "accompanied by the prescribed application and fee...."

After the deposit is received and transferred to another service unit of the Library for its collections or other disposition, it is no longer available to the Copyright Office. If you wish to register the work, you must deposit additional copies or phonorecords with your application and fee.

Renewal Registration

To register a renewal, send:

1. A properly completed application Form RE and, if necessary, Form RE Addendum, and

2. A nonrefundable filing fee of $45 without Addendum; $60 with Addendum for each application. (See Note above.) Each Addendum form must be accompanied by a deposit representing the work being reviewed. See Circular 15, "Renewal of Copyright."

NOTE: *Complete the application form using black ink pen or type.* You may photocopy blank application forms. *However*, photocopied forms submitted to the Copyright Office must be clear, legible, on a good grade of 8-1/2 inch by 11-inch white paper suitable for automatic feeding through a photocopier. The forms should be printed, preferably in black ink, head-to-head so that when you turn the sheet over, the top of page 2 is directly behind the top of page 1. *Forms not meeting these requirements may be returned resulting in delayed registration.*

Special Deposit Requirements

Special deposit requirements exist for many types of works. The following are prominent examples of exceptions to the general deposit requirements:

+ If the work is a motion picture, the deposit requirement is one complete copy of the unpublished or published motion picture and a separate written description of its contents, such as a continuity, press book, or synopsis.

+ If the work is a literary, dramatic, or musical work *published only in a phonorecord*, the deposit requirement is one complete phonorecord.

+ If the work is an unpublished or published computer program, the deposit requirement is one visually perceptible copy in source code of the *first 25 and last 25 pages* of the program. For a program of fewer than 50 pages, the deposit is a copy of the entire program. For more information on computer program registration, including deposits for revised programs and provisions for trade secrets, request "Copyright Registration for Computer Programs" [http://www.loc.gov/copyright/circs/circ61.pdf].

+ If the work is in a CD-ROM format, the deposit requirement is one complete copy of the material, that is, the CD-ROM, the operating software, and any manual(s) accompanying it. If registration is sought for the computer program on the CD-ROM, the deposit should also include a printout of the first 25 and last 25 pages of source code for the program.

In the case of works reproduced in three-dimensional copies, identifying material such as photographs or drawings is ordinarily required. Other examples of special deposit requirements (but by no means an exhaustive list) include many works of the visual arts such as greeting cards, toys, fabrics, oversized materials (request "Deposit Requirements for Registration of Claims to Copyright in Visual Arts Material" [http://www.loc.gov/copyright/circs/circ40a.pdf]); video games and other machine-readable audiovisual works (request Circular 61 [http://www.loc.gov/copyright/circs/circ61.pdf]); automated databases (request Circular 65 [http://www.loc.gov/copyright/circs/circ65.pdf] , "Copyright Registration for Automated Databases"); and contributions to collective works. For information about deposit requirements for group registration of serials, request Circular 62 "Copyright Registration for Serials." [http://www.loc.gov/copyright/circs/circ62.pdf] ,

If you are unsure of the deposit requirement for your work, write or call the Copyright Office and describe the work you wish to register.

Unpublished Collections

Under the following conditions, a work may be registered in unpublished form as a "collection," with one application form and one fee:

+ The elements of the collection are assembled in an orderly form;

+ The combined elements bear a single title identifying the collection
  as a whole;
  + The copyright claimant in all the elements and in the collection as
  a whole is the same; and
+ All the elements are by the same author, or, if they are by different authors,
at least one of the authors has contributed copyrightable authorship to each
element. An unpublished collection is not indexed under the individual titles
of the contents but under the title of the collection.

NOTE: A *Library of Congress Catalog Card Number* is different from a
copyright registration number. The Cataloging in Publication (CIP) Division
of the Library of Congress is responsible for assigning LC Catalog Card
Numbers and is operationally separate from the Copyright Office. A book may
be registered in or deposited with the Copyright Office but not necessarily
cataloged and added to the Library's collections. For information about
obtaining an LC Catalog Card Number, see the following homepage:
[http://lcweb2.loc.gov/pcn]. For information on International Standard Book
Numbering (ISBN), write to: ISBN, R. R. Bowker, 121 Chanlon Road, New
Providence, NJ 07974. Call (877) 310-7333. For further information and to
apply online, see [http://www.bowker.com/standards/]. For information on
International Standard Serial Numbering (ISSN), write to: Library of Congress,
National Serials Data Program, Serial Record Division, Washington, D. C.
20540-4160. Call (202) 707-6452. Or obtain information from
[http://www.loc.gov/issn/].

EFFECTIVE DATE OF REGISTRATION

*A copyright registration is effective on the date the Copyright Office receives
all the required elements in acceptable form*, regardless of how long it then
takes to process the application and mail the certificate of registration. The
time the Copyright Office requires to process an application varies, depending
on the amount of material the Office is receiving.

If you apply for copyright registration, you will not receive an acknowledgment
that your application has been received (the Office receives more than 600,000
applications annually), but you can expect:

+ A letter or a telephone call from a Copyright Office staff member if further
information is needed or

+ A certificate of registration indicating that the work has been registered, or if the application cannot be accepted, a letter explaining why it has been rejected.

Requests to have certificates available for pickup in the Public Information Office or to have certificates sent by Federal Express or another mail service cannot be honored.

If you want to know the date that the Copyright Office receives your material, send it by registered or certified mail and request a return receipt.

CORRECTIONS AND AMPLIFICATIONS OF EXISTING REGISTRATIONS

To correct an error in a copyright registration or to amplify the information given in a registration, file a supplementary registration form — Form CA [http://www.loc.gov/copyright/forms/formca.pdf] — with the Copyright Office. The filing fee is $65. (See Note above.) The information in a supplementary registration augments but does not supersede that contained in the earlier registration. Note also that a supplementary registration is not a substitute for an original registration, for a renewal registration, or for recording a transfer of ownership. For further information about supplementary registration, request Circular 8 "Supplementary Copyright Registration" [http://www.loc.gov/copyright/circs/circ08.pdf].

MANDATORY DEPOSIT FOR WORKS PUBLISHED IN THE UNITED STATES

Although a copyright registration is not required, the Copyright Act establishes a mandatory deposit requirement for works published in the United States. See the definition of "publication." In general, the owner of copyright or the owner of the exclusive right of publication in the work has a legal obligation to deposit in the Copyright Office, within 3 months of publication in the United States, two copies (or in the case of sound recordings, two phonorecords) for the use of the Library of Congress. Failure to make the deposit can result in fines and other penalties but does not affect copyright protection.

Certain categories of works are exempt entirely from the mandatory deposit requirements, and the obligation is reduced for certain other categories. For further information about mandatory deposit, request Circular 7d "Mandatory Deposit of Copies or Phonorecords for the Library of Congress." [http://www.loc.gov/copyright/circs/circ07d.pdf].

USE OF MANDATORY DEPOSIT TO SATISFY REGISTRATION REQUIREMENTS

For works published in the United States, the copyright law contains a provision under which a single deposit can be made to satisfy both the deposit requirements for the Library and the registration requirements. In order to have this dual effect, the copies or phonorecords must be accompanied by the prescribed application form and filing fee.

WHO MAY FILE AN APPLICATION FORM?

The following persons are legally entitled to submit an application form:

+ *The author*. This is either the person who actually created the work or, if the work was made for hire, the employer or other person for whom the work was prepared.

+ *The copyright claimant*. The copyright claimant is defined in Copyright Office regulations as either the author of the work or a person or organization that has obtained ownership of all the rights under the copyright initially belonging to the author. This category includes a person or organization who has obtained by contract the right to claim legal title to the copyright in an application for copyright registration.

+ *The owner of exclusive right(s)*. Under the law, any of the exclusive rights that make up a copyright and any subdivision of them can be transferred and owned separately, even though the transfer may be limited in time or place of effect. The term "copyright owner" with respect to any one of the exclusive rights contained in a copyright refers to the owner of that particular right. Any owner of an exclusive right may apply for registration of a claim in the work.

+ *The duly authorized agent* of such author, other copyright claimant, or owner of exclusive right(s). Any person authorized to act on behalf of the author, other copyright claimant, or owner of exclusive rights may apply for registration.

There is no requirement that applications be prepared or filed by an attorney.

APPLICATION FORMS

For Original Registration

Form PA [http://www.loc.gov/copyright/forms/formpai.pdf] for published and unpublished works of the performing arts (musical and dramatic works, pantomimes and choreographic works, motion pictures and other audiovisual works)

Form SE [http://www.loc.gov/copyright/forms/formsei.pdf]

for serials, works issued or intended to be issued in successive parts bearing numerical or chronological designations and intended to be continued indefinitely (periodicals, newspapers, magazines, newsletters, annuals, journals, etc.)

Form SR [http://www.loc.gov/copyright/forms/formsri.pdf]

for published and unpublished sound recordings

Form TX [http://www.loc.gov/copyright/forms/formtxi.pdf]

for published and unpublished nondramatic literary works

Form VA [http://www.loc.gov/copyright/forms/formvai.pdf]

for published and unpublished works of the visual arts (pictorial, graphic, and sculptural works, including architectural works)

Form G/DN [http://www.loc.gov/copyright/forms/formgdn.pdf]

  a specialized form to register a complete month's issues of a daily
  newspaper when certain conditions are met

Short Form SE [http://www.loc.gov/copyright/forms/formses.pdf], and
Short Form SE Group [http://www.loc.gov/copyright/forms/formseg.pdf]
specialized SE forms for use when certain requirements are met

Short Form TX [http://www.loc.gov/copyright/forms/formtxs.pdf],
Short Form PA [http://www.loc.gov/copyright/forms/formpas.pdf], and
Short Form VA [http://www.loc.gov/copyright/forms/formvas.pdf]
  short versions of applications for original registration. For further
  information about using the short forms, request publication SL-7.
Form GATT [http://www.loc.gov/copyright/forms/formgatt.pdf], and
Form GATT/GRP [http://www.loc.gov/copyright/forms/formgatg.pdf]
specialized forms to register a claim in a work or group of related works in
which U. S. copyright was restored under the 1994 Uruguay Round
Agreements Act (URAA). For further information, request Circular 38b
[http://www.loc.gov/copyright/circs/circ38b.pdf].

*** For Renewal Registration

Form RE [http://www.loc.gov/copyright/forms/formrei.pdf]

for claims to renew copyright in works copyrighted under the law in effect
through December 31, 1977 (1909 Copyright Act) and registered during the
initial 28-year copyright term

Form RE Addendum [http://www.loc.gov/copyright/forms/formrea.pdf]

accompanies Form RE for claims to renew copyright in works copyrighted
under the 1909 Copyright Act but never registered during their initial 28-year
copyright term

*** For Corrections and Amplifications

Form CA [http://www.loc.gov/copyright/forms/formca.pdf]

for supplementary registration to correct or amplify information given in the
Copyright Office record of an earlier registration

*** For a Group of Contributions to Periodicals

Form GR/CP [http://www.loc.gov/copyright/forms/formgrcp.pdf]

an adjunct application to be used for registration of a group of contributions to periodicals in addition to an application Form TX, PA, or VA

*** How to Obtain Application Forms

See "For Further Information" below.

You must have Adobe Acrobat Reader (R) [http://www.adobe.com/prodindex/acrobat/readstep.html] installed on your computer to view and print the forms accessed on the Internet. Adobe Acrobat Reader may be downloaded free from Adobe Systems Incorporated through links from the same Internet site from which the forms are available.

Print forms head to head (top of page 2 is directly behind the top of page 1) on a single piece of good quality, 8-1/2-inch by 11-inch white paper. To achieve the best quality copies of the application forms, use a laser printer.

*** FILL-IN FORMS AVAILABLE

All Copyright Office forms are available on the Copyright Office Website in fill-in version. Go to http://www.loc.gov/copyright/forms/ and follow the instructions. The fill-in forms allow you to enter information while the form is displayed on the screen by an Adobe Acrobat Reader product. You may then print the completed form and mail it to the Copyright Office. Fill-in forms provide a clean, sharp printout for your records and for filing with the Copyright Office.

FEES

All remittances should be in the form of drafts, that is, checks, money orders, or bank drafts, payable to: Register of Copyrights. Do not send cash. Drafts must be redeemable without service or exchange fee through a U. S. institution, must be payable in U. S. dollars, and must be imprinted with American Banking Association routing numbers. International Money Orders and Postal Money Orders that are negotiable only at a post office are not acceptable.

If a check received in payment of the filing fee is returned to the Copyright Office as uncollectible, the Copyright Office will cancel the registration and will notify the remitter.

The filing fee for processing an original, supplementary, or renewal claim is nonrefundable, whether or not copyright registration is ultimately made.

Do not send cash. The Copyright Office cannot assume any responsibility for the loss of currency sent in payment of copyright fees. For further information, request Circular 4 "Copyright Fees" [http://www.loc.gov/copyright/circs/circ04.pdf].

NOTE: Copyright Office fees are subject to change. For current fees, please check the Copyright Office Website at http://www.loc.gov/copyright/, write the Copyright Office, or call (202) 707-3000.

SEARCH OF COPYRIGHT OFFICE RECORDS

The records of the Copyright Office are open for inspection and searching by the public. Moreover, on request, the Copyright Office will search its records for you at the statutory hourly rate of $65 for each hour or fraction of an hour. (See NOTE above.) For information on searching the Office records concerning the copyright status or ownership of a work, request "How to Investigate the Copyright Status of a Work" [http://www.loc.gov/copyright/circs/circ22.pdf], and "The Copyright Card Catalog and the Online Files of the Copyright Office" [http://www.loc.gov/copyright/circs/circ23.pdf].

Copyright Office records in machine-readable form cataloged from January 1, 1978, to the present, including registration and renewal information and recorded documents, are now available for searching on the Internet. These files may be examined through LOCIS (Library of Congress Information System). You may connect to LOCIS through the World Wide Web at [http://www.loc.gov/copyright/rb.html]

FOR FURTHER INFORMATION

Information via the Internet: Circulars, announcements, regulations, other related materials, and all copyright application forms are available from the Copyright Office Website at http://www.loc.gov/copyright/.

Information by fax: Circulars and other information (but not application forms) are available from Fax-on-Demand at (202) 707-2600.

Information by telephone: For general information about copyright, call the Copyright Public Information Office at (202) 707-3000. The TTY number is (202) 707-6737. Information specialists are on duty from 8:30 a. m. to 5:00 p. m. Monday through Friday, eastern time, except federal holidays. Recorded information is available 24 hours a day. Or, if you know which application forms and circulars you want, request them from the Forms and Publications Hotline at (202) 707-9100 24 hours a day. Leave a recorded message.

Information by regular mail: Write to:

Library of Congress
Copyright Office
Publications Section, LM-455
101 Independence Avenue, S.E.
Washington, D.C. 20559-6000
For a list of other material published by the Copyright Office, request Circular 2 "Publications on Copyright" [http://www.loc.gov/copyright/circs/circ02.pdf].

The Copyright Office provides a free electronic mailing list, *NewsNet,* that issues periodic email messages on the subject of copyright. The messages alert subscribers to hearings, deadlines for comments, new and proposed regulations, new publications, and other copyright-related subjects of interest. NewsNet is not an interactive discussion group. To subscribe, send a message to listserv@rs8.loc.gov. In the body of the message say: SUBSCRIBE USCOPYRIGHT. You will receive a standard welcoming message indicating that your subscription to *NewsNet* has been accepted.

The Copyright Public Information Office is open to the public 8:30 a.m. to 5:00 p.m. Monday through Friday, eastern time, except federal holidays. The office is located in the Library of Congress, James Madison Memorial Building, Room 401, at 101 Independence Avenue, S.E., Washington, D.C., near the Capitol South Metro stop. Information specialists are available to answer questions, provide circulars, and accept applications for registration. Access for disabled individuals is at the front door on Independence Avenue, S.E.

The Copyright Office is not permitted to give legal advice. If information or guidance is needed on matters such as disputes over the ownership of a copyright, suits against possible infringers, the procedure for getting a work published, or the method of obtaining royalty payments, it may be necessary to consult an attorney

Library of Congress
Copyright Office
101 Independence Avenue, S. E.
Washington, D.C. 20559-6000
http://www.loc.gov/copyright/

——————————————————————— Rev: December 2000

Format Note:

This electronic version has been altered slightly from the original printed text for presentation on the World Wide Web. For a copy of the original circular, consult the Circular 1 pdf version [http://www.loc.gov/copyright/circs/circ01.pdf], or write to Copyright Office, 101 Independence Avenue S.E., Washington, D.C. 20559-6000.

Note from the Editor.

Odin's Library Classics strives to bring you unedited and unabridged works of classical literature. As such this is the complete and unabridged version of the original. The English language has evolved since the writing and some of the words appear in their original form, or at least the form most commonly used at the time. This is done to protect the original intent of the author. If at any time you are unsure of the meaning of the original meaning of a word, please do your research on that word. It is important to preserve the history of the English language.

Taylor Anderson

9 781976 356971